More Than
Sisters,
We Are Also Friends

ISBN: 978-1-59842-868-1

Wonderful Wacky Women®

Inspiring•Uplifting•Empowering

is a trademark of Suzy and Al Toronto. Used under license.

█ and Blue Mountain Press are registered in U.S. Patent and Trademark Office. Certain trademarks are used under license.

Printed in China.
First Printing: 2015

♻ This book is printed on recycled paper.

This book is printed on paper that has been specially produced to be acid free (neutral pH) and contains no groundwood or unbleached pulp. It conforms with the requirements of the American National Standards Institute, Inc., so as to ensure that this book will last and be enjoyed by future generations.

Blue Mountain Arts, Inc.
P.O. Box 4549, Boulder, Colorado 80306

More Than
Sisters,
We Are Also Friends

Suzy Toronto

Blue Mountain Press™
Boulder, Colorado

What are the infinite chances
that of all the zillions of people in the world,
God would see fit to make the two of us sisters?

The common bond between us
goes far beyond mere bloodlines.
We find joy in each other's triumphs
and sorrow in each other's pain.
We share a sibling intimacy
that defies description…
a family connection
that forever binds us to each other.

But the greatest miracle of all
is a blessing I will never take lightly.
Beyond the connections, the bloodlines,
and all the family ties,
we are so much more than sisters.
Between us is a relationship
more rare and precious than any worldly treasure…
for we are also friends.

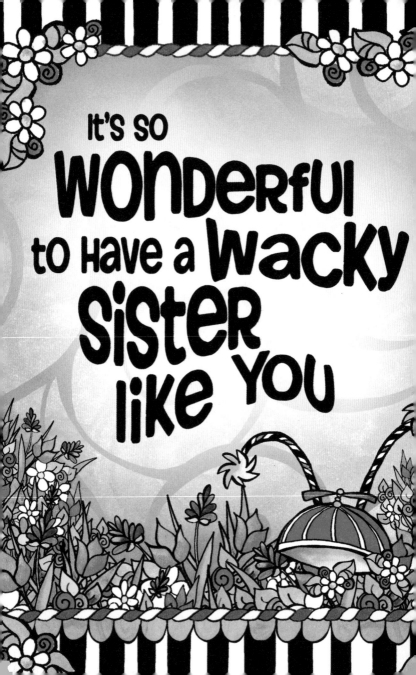

We are alike in so many ways,
yet different in so many others.
It seems to give a wonderful balance
to the sometimes wild, wacky lives we lead.

Whether we are giggling, whining, or crying,
we always seem to have a good time doing it.
We have more fun than anyone should be allowed to,
which validates that maybe, just maybe,
our wacky lives are normal after all.

But what I really love about us are our differences.
You are strong when I am not,
you are levelheaded when I'm feeling a bit off balance,
and you lift me up when I think I can't go on.

And then, the icing on the cake...
you put up with the very worst of me
because deep down inside,
you know the best of me is worth the hassle!

What a match we make!
Two wild, wacky, wonderful women
riding together in the front seat
of the roller coaster of life...
and having the time of our lives!

And I can't think of anyone
I'd rather do it with.

©Suzy Toronto

We are proof positive that the nuts
don't fall far from the tree in our family orchard!
But wacky as we are,
our roots bind us strong and eternal.
Unbreakable and always forgiving,
our wacky sisterhood has endured
even the most challenging trials.
Our family and upbringing give us a closeness
that defies description.
I know you will always be there for me,
and you know I am forever here for you.
For that I will always feel blessed.

What's even better is now that we are older,
I realize what a great friend you are as well.
How wonderful to share so much history
and know each other so intimately
that our conversations never
need a preface for explanation!
We can stop midsentence
and the other one can finish the story.
Such a blessing. Such a closeness.
Such a friendship.
And, best of all,
such a true and eternal sisterhood.

© Suzy Toronto

Over the years, we've dealt with
sibling rivalry and survived.
We've teased each other until tears
stained one or both of our cheeks,
and we lived to laugh about it.
And if we each had a nickel for all the times
we pretended as kids that
we didn't even know each other…
well, we could both retire rich!

But now, all that aside,
I truly love that we are sisters.
We have shared so much over the years,
and the good and bad have bonded us
with a sibling intimacy that is unbreakable.
I hope you know how
very much you mean to me
and that I love you a whole bunch!
I think you are an amazing woman
and a wonderful sister.
The older we get, the more I appreciate
how blessed I am to have you in my life.

© Suzy Toronto

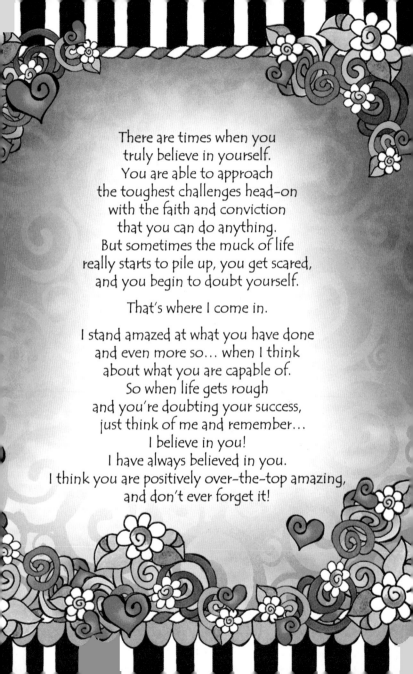

There are times when you
truly believe in yourself.
You are able to approach
the toughest challenges head-on
with the faith and conviction
that you can do anything.
But sometimes the muck of life
really starts to pile up, you get scared,
and you begin to doubt yourself.

That's where I come in.

I stand amazed at what you have done
and even more so… when I think
about what you are capable of.
So when life gets rough
and you're doubting your success,
just think of me and remember…
I believe in you!
I have always believed in you.
I think you are positively over-the-top amazing,
and don't ever forget it!

You light up a room
with your presence.
You listen and you hear.

You know when to push
and when to shove.
But most important,
you know when to back off!

You are comfort.
You are compassion.
You are heart and soul combined
in a most glorious package…

And you bring me such joy!

© Suzy Toronto

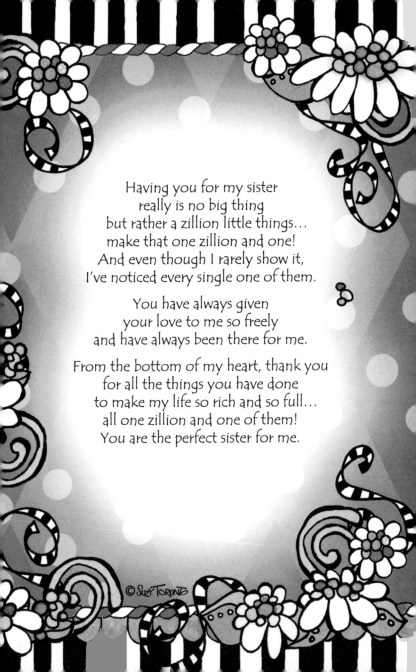

Having you for my sister
really is no big thing
but rather a zillion little things…
make that one zillion and one!
And even though I rarely show it,
I've noticed every single one of them.

You have always given
your love to me so freely
and have always been there for me.

From the bottom of my heart, thank you
for all the things you have done
to make my life so rich and so full…
all one zillion and one of them!
You are the perfect sister for me.

© Suzy Toronto

Two Wonderful Sisters...

One Wacky Heart

It's true, our wild, wacky hearts
are tied to each other,
bound by a family closeness
that only siblings can have.
Our upbringing has made us
alike in so many ways,
but it's not only the similarities
that make our relationship great...
it's the differences as well.

Some days we feel like we come
from totally different planets,
and then the next moment,
we are practically reading each other's mind.
And then there are those times
we claim to have different styles
and show up wearing virtually the same thing.

It's a yin-and-yang thing…
so different and so alike,
yet the perfect complement for each other.
But what I really love most
are those moments of pristine clarity,
when we recognize almost simultaneously
that both of us are better for it.
It's a cool thing that only sisters like us experience.

The bottom line is this: our being siblings
doesn't simply bind us heart to heart
but between us creates one heart…
each of us is half of a whole that
together is an unbreakable sisterhood.

©Suzy Toronto

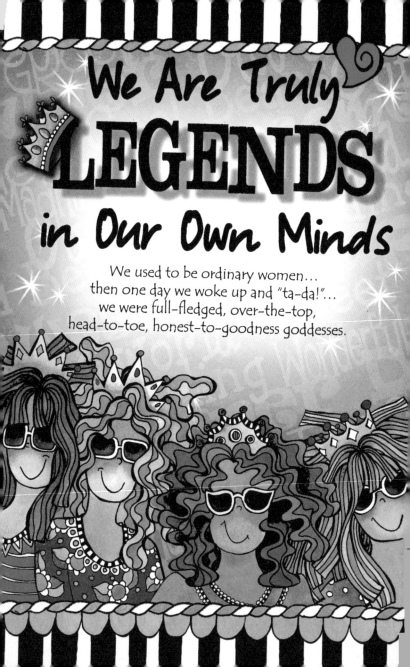

We Are Truly LEGENDS in Our Own Minds

We used to be ordinary women…
then one day we woke up and "ta-da!"…
we were full-fledged, over-the-top,
head-to-toe, honest-to-goodness goddesses.

We didn't physically change on the outside,
but a magnificent transformation
took place on the inside.
Looking in the mirror,
we suddenly realized we were finally at peace
with everything about ourselves...
every curve of our bodies, every wave in our hair.
We now see ourselves as the sensuous
and radiant beings we truly are.

Oh yeah, there is no doubt about it.
We are legends in our own minds!

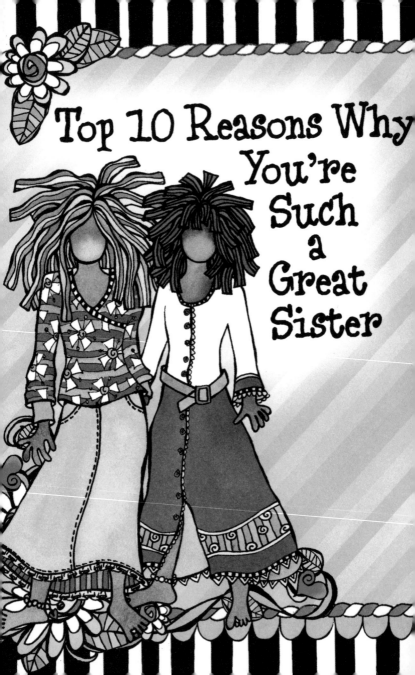

#10 You know all my history, so I don't have to explain myself when we talk.

#9 You immediately forgive my extensive and expensive shortcomings.

#8 You lift me up when I am down and knock me down when I am too full of myself.

#7 You are the president of my fan club, even though I don't have one.

#6 You tell me the truth when I ask if I look fat, and you lie when I get a bad haircut.

#5 You never criticize my weight, my messy house, or my dirty car.

#4 You accept our wacky family, and so do I, even though they make us crazy.

#3 You never roll your eyes at my insecurities.

#2 You understand that chocolate can solve all my problems.

And the #1 reason why you're such a great sister:
 you know all about me,
  and you've got my back anyway.

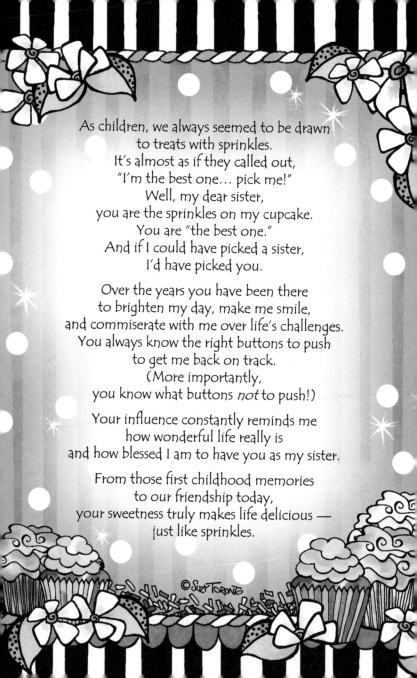

As children, we always seemed to be drawn
to treats with sprinkles.
It's almost as if they called out,
"I'm the best one... pick me!"
Well, my dear sister,
you are the sprinkles on my cupcake.
You are "the best one."
And if I could have picked a sister,
I'd have picked you.

Over the years you have been there
to brighten my day, make me smile,
and commiserate with me over life's challenges.
You always know the right buttons to push
to get me back on track.
(More importantly,
you know what buttons *not* to push!)

Your influence constantly reminds me
how wonderful life really is
and how blessed I am to have you as my sister.

From those first childhood memories
to our friendship today,
your sweetness truly makes life delicious —
just like sprinkles.

©Suzy Toronto

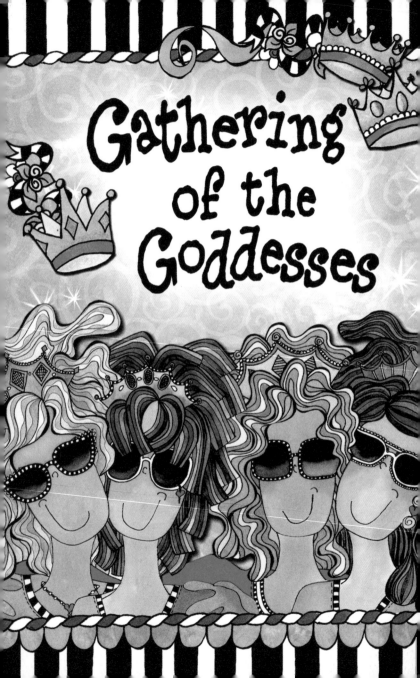

Gathering of the Goddesses

It is a known fact
that goddesses attract other goddesses.
You know, "Birds of a feather…"
But the really cool thing is that quite often
they flock together long before they reach
their true lofty status of "goddess."
By the time they become goddesses,
they've been gathering together for so long —
giving, sharing, loving, and caring —
that they know intimate details
about one another's lives…
making their bond unbreakable.

Whether shopping, going out to lunch,
lounging over pedicures, or sitting on the beach,
a gathering of goddesses can't be missed.
Just listen for the buzz of conversation,
the tears of shared sorrows,
and the fits of irrepressible laughter.
You'll know in a minute
you're in the presence of greatness.

© Suzy Toronto

If I could be there right now,
I'd wrap both my arms around you so tight,
and I'd never let you go.
I'd be like one of those "long huggers"
who hug way past
the point of your comfort zone.

I'd hug you until you felt
all the wonderful, warm, and
fuzzy feelings I have for you.
Then I'd start telling you
how totally amazing you are.
I'd ramble on and on about
all the greatness
and courage I see in you.
I'm sure you'd roll your eyes
and gasp for air,
but I wouldn't let that stop me.
I'd just go on and on.

It's not that my hug and
ramblings would solve anything,
but they would sure
make me feel better.

©Suzy Toronto

Sometimes the miles between us
make me feel like we're worlds apart.
It's such a foreign feeling compared to
the years we spent growing up side by side —
always together, never any separation.
But now, so many years later,
those miles can really start to get me down.

So when I'm missing you,
I stop and remember that what we have
transcends the miles
and how when we do connect,
whether with a note or a phone call,
our sisterhood instantly erases the distance.

It's a feeling of such irrepressible comfort
that can only come when two people
have shared so much, for so long,
and understand each other
on such a deep and profound level.
What we have is so much stronger
than friendship.

We are sisters…
connected heart to heart.

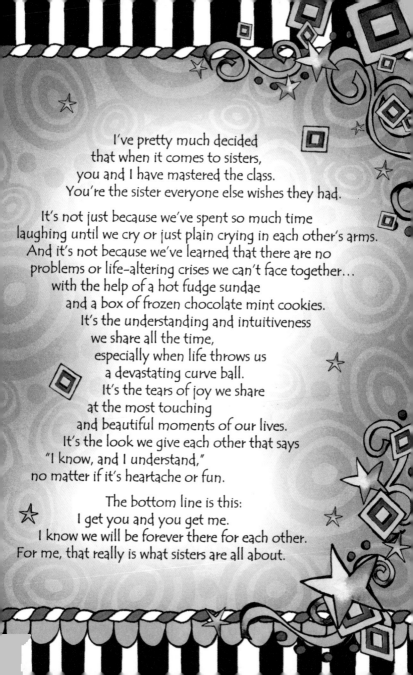

I've pretty much decided
that when it comes to sisters,
you and I have mastered the class.
You're the sister everyone else wishes they had.

It's not just because we've spent so much time
laughing until we cry or just plain crying in each other's arms.
And it's not because we've learned that there are no
problems or life-altering crises we can't face together…
with the help of a hot fudge sundae
and a box of frozen chocolate mint cookies.
It's the understanding and intuitiveness
we share all the time,
especially when life throws us
a devastating curve ball.
It's the tears of joy we share
at the most touching
and beautiful moments of our lives.
It's the look we give each other that says
"I know, and I understand,"
no matter if it's heartache or fun.

The bottom line is this:
I get you and you get me.
I know we will be forever there for each other.
For me, that really is what sisters are all about.

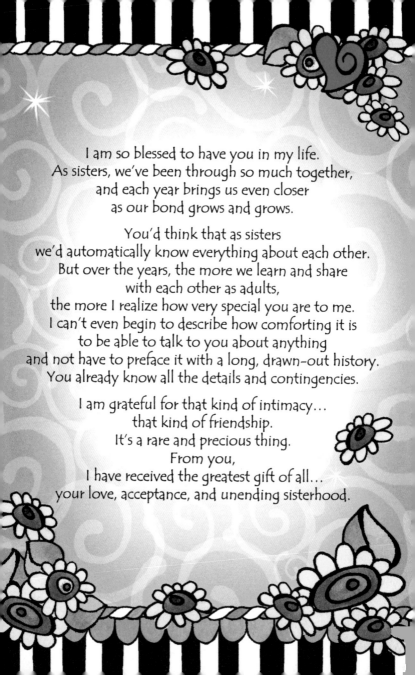

I am so blessed to have you in my life.
As sisters, we've been through so much together,
and each year brings us even closer
as our bond grows and grows.

You'd think that as sisters
we'd automatically know everything about each other.
But over the years, the more we learn and share
with each other as adults,
the more I realize how very special you are to me.
I can't even begin to describe how comforting it is
to be able to talk to you about anything
and not have to preface it with a long, drawn-out history.
You already know all the details and contingencies.

I am grateful for that kind of intimacy…
that kind of friendship.
It's a rare and precious thing.
From you,
I have received the greatest gift of all…
your love, acceptance, and unending sisterhood.

I simply can't imagine my world without you in it.
Together we feel each other's joy
and share each other's pain
with a connection that only sisters could have.

We can talk openly anytime,
knowing our most intimate
conversations will be kept safe,
with a confidence that cannot be breached.
The bond of our sisterhood anchors us
with a solidarity that allows us to
ride out any storm.

But the greatest blessing of all
is that through all the ups and downs,
all the trials and heartaches we have endured,
we can always find solace and peace
when we are together…
a level of comfort like no other.
I am forever grateful
that our relationship is a sisterhood
of unconditional love and friendship
that truly makes my heart tingle.

© Suzy Toronto

The true test for siblings is to make it through
childhood and still love each other.
Together we survived
growing pains, sibling rivalry,
teasing, Dad's lectures, and Mom's cooking.
We made it through the "love you, hate you" stages
and emerged with an
"I know all your secrets yet promise
never to blackmail you" kind of bond.

You really are the only person
I can call at 4:00 a.m.
who will come running
with arms and heart wide open…
no questions asked.
You can always count on me,
and I can always count on you.
You always know what I need…
even if it's a good, swift kick!

We are forever family, and I love you, Sis,
with all my heart and soul.
I am so glad you are my sister…
forever, for always, and no matter what.

© Suzy Toronto

About the Author

So this is me… I'm a tad wacky and just shy of crazy. I'm fiftysomething and live in the sleepy village of Tangerine, Florida, with my husband, Al, and a big, goofy dog named Lucy. And because life wasn't crazy enough, my eightysomething-year-old parents live with us too. (In my home, the nuts don't fall far from the tree!) I eat far too much chocolate, and I drink sparkling water by the gallon. I practice yoga, ride a little red scooter, and go to the beach every chance I get. I have five grown children and over a dozen grandkids who love me as much as I adore them. I teach them to dip their French fries in their chocolate shakes and to make up any old words to the tunes they like. But most of all, I teach them to never, ever color inside the lines. This is the Wild Wacky Wonderful life I lead, and I wouldn't have it any other way. Welcome to my world!